IRISH WISDOM
FOR PARENTS

Library of Congress Cataloging-in-Publication Data:

Pritty, Mandy.

Irish wisdom for parents / illustrated by Mandy Pritty

80 p.   12.7 x 17.7 cm.

ISBN 0-8118-3112-4

1. Proverbs, Irish. 2. Parenting—Quotations, maxims, etc. I. Title.

PN6505.C5 P75 2002

398.9'21'09417—dc21   2001037157

Printed in Singapore

Designed by Lucy Nielsen

Typeset in Nicolas Cochin and Dorchester Script

Distributed in Canada by Raincoast Books

9050 Shaughnessy Street

Vancouver, British Columbia V6P 6E5

10 9 8 7 6 5 4 3 2 1

Chronicle Books LLC

85 Second Street

San Francisco, California 94105

www.chroniclebooks.com

Irish Wisdom
for Parents

illustrated by MANDY PRITTY

CHRONICLE BOOKS
SAN FRANCISCO

Every mother thinks it's for her own
child the sun rises.

The lucky person has only to be born.

Be good to the child and he will come
to you tomorrow.

You've got to do your own growing, no matter how tall your grandfather was.

Reputation is more enduring than life.

The tree remains, but not the hand
that planted it.

What will come from the briar
but the berry?

Nature is stronger than nurture.

Every branch blossoms according to the
root from which it is sprung.

Whether it be black, dun, or brown,
it is its own kid the goat loves.

To the raven her own chick is white.

Every bird thinks her own young ones
the handsomest in the wood.

By degrees the castles are built.

Bend the sapling while it is young.

Praise the young and they will flourish.

Every nursling as he is nursed.

Do not go between the tree and its bark.

A mangy colt often turns into a fine horse.

A good beginning is half the work.

The lamb is a sheep in the long run.

A child must creep before he walks.

One look before is better than
   two behind.

Wisdom does not come before age.

If children won't make you laugh,
they won't make you cry.

The soft twig is more durable than
the stubborn tree.

Cleverness is better than strength.

You can't put an old head on
young shoulders.

In youth we have our troubles before us,
in age we have our pleasures behind us.

An old child has a long memory.

It's hard to teach an old dog to dance.

Young people don't know what age is, and
old people forget what youth was.

The schoolhouse bell sounds bitter in youth and sweet in old age.

Questioning is the door of knowledge.

Knowledge comes through practice.

There is no luck except where
there is discipline.

Better good manners than good looks.

Handsome is as handsome does.

Cleanliness is part of glory.

A child will be known by its manners.

Comb your hair and you're
    halfway there.

Watching is part of good play.

What the child sees is what the
child does.

As the old cock crows, the young
cock learns.

Every bird goes along with its own flock.

The young crab has the same walk
  as the old crab.

The nature of the cat shows in its eyes.

The mother's failings will naturally
be seen in the daughter.

A wild goose never reared a tame gosling.

A dropped stitch is soon a hole.

Every bird according to his rearing.

What can you expect from a pig
   but a grunt?

What should you expect from a cat
   but a kitten?

It is natural for the fawn of a deer
to have fleetness.

The young seal takes naturally
to the sea.

Youth likes to wander.

Every dog is a pup until he hunts.

Youth does not mind where it sets its foot.

The young shed many skins.

Often a cow does not take after its breed.

A bird flies away from every brood.

The youngest thorns are the sharpest.

The older the worse—like the fox's cubs.

A child that's left to himself will put
his mother to shame.

A busy mother makes a lazy daughter.

Street angel, house devil.

Many is the upright tree with a branch
as crooked as can be.

Every finger has not the same length,
nor every son the same disposition.

Better a son who gambles than a son
who drinks.

There is no anguish of soul until one
has children.

A wise son makes a father glad but a
foolish son is a mother's sorrow.

It is the children of the fortunate who make the unfortunate people.

A son like the mother, and a daughter like the father.

Whatever else might come to pass, you
won't make a racehorse of an ass.

What would a young cat do but eat mice?

Empty vessels make the most noise.

Hear much, say little.

The young and the foolish are the
hardest to teach.

A silent mouth never did any harm.

They are scarce of news that speak
ill of their mother.

The silent are often guilty.

Don't tell secrets to the children of
your own relatives.

The three rudenesses of this world:
youth mocking old age, health
mocking at sickness, and a wise
man mocking a fool.

One rotten apple rots a bagful.

There are two tellings to every story.

A soft answer turns away anger.

A sweet voice does not injure the teeth.

A little of anything isn't worth a pin; but
a wee bit of sense is worth a lot.

Everyone is wise till he speaks.

Little pigs have big ears.

The child fears, the man hates.

A handful of skill is better than
a bagful of gold.

Better have no cow than no son.

The best horse doesn't always
win the race.

No man ever wore a cravat as nice as his own child's arm around his neck.

Love a woman or a child without
their knowing it.

If you love the mother, you love
her brood.

The three loveliest sights to see: a garden
of white potatoes in blossom, a ship
under sail, and a wife after giving birth.

There was never a scabby sheep
in a flock that didn't like to
have a companion.

A boy's best friend is his mother.

Every man is a lion over what
   is his own.

&

Your son is your son until he marries,
   but your daughter is your daughter
   until you die.

&

Baptize your own child first.

A house with no cat, dog, or child
is a house without love.

Blood is thicker than water.

What is in the marrow is hard to take
out of the bone.

A king's son is not nobler than his food.

Every terrier is bold in the doorway
of its own house.

A new broom sweeps clean, but the old
brush knows the corners.

Don't build the sty before the
litter comes.

The biggest help is help and even the
smallest help is help.

Patience is a plaster for every wound.

Truth stands when everything else falls.

Sense doesn't come before age.

Wisdom is often hard.

A child without a star, a hearth
without a child.

It is not the big mansion that makes
the happy home.

Good humor comes from the kitchen.

There's no hearth like your own hearth.

To know somebody you must live in
the same house with him.

A good laugh and a long sleep—the best cures of all.

The stars make no noise.

Greatness knows gentleness.

Youth cannot believe.

There's no love until there's a family.